*Life can only be understood backwards,
but must be lived forwards.*

Sören Kierkegaard

A Bit of Thanks

I've learned so much from the people who have walked beside me in my life, and I am thankful for each person who has left an imprint on my soul and a memory in my heart...

Thanks, Mom and Dad, for allowing me to make my own mistakes, and for padding my falls with love and understanding. I want to thank my girls for giving me friendships that will last lifetimes and for always being there, even when I wasn't. And though I never thought I'd say this, I want to thank the many boyfriends who have broken my heart. I am stronger and wiser for having known you. To my sister... I've learned all I know from you and will continue to squish mashed potatoes through my teeth with pride.

Being a Teen

Words of Advice from Someone Who's Been There

Diane Mastromarino

Blue Mountain Press™
Boulder, Colorado

The publisher wishes to acknowledge and thank Virginia Nowell for creating the illustrations that appear in this book, as well as the SPS Studios creative staff.

ISBN: 0-88396-626-3

ACKNOWLEDGMENTS appear on page 78.

Manufactured in the United States of America.
Third printing: 2003

Blue Mountain Arts, Inc.
P.O. Box 4549, Boulder, Colorado 80306

the buzz...

I Did It...

I somehow survived my teen years and now stand on the edge of adulthood with a pen in my hand. Though I'd rather not look back, I feel the need to tell you that it really wasn't as bad as it seemed, that I cried over spilled milk many more times than I should have, that I did pass my driving test (eventually), and that the bad haircut that branded me "onion head"...well actually, that really was that bad. As I leave my teenage years behind, I leave this book as a constant reminder of what NOT to do upon entering those wonderful years of "teenhood." If nothing else, by reading this, you'll get a good laugh — not to mention the enjoyment of some great quotations and poetry, some written by teens and others by renowned authors.

I'm sure as a teenager you are tired of hearing the chorus of monotonous voices telling you what you should be doing. We need to make our own mistakes. Everyone does; it's part of the learning process. We are told what to do, yet we make opposite choices, which many times are the wrong ones. We can do without the "I told you so's," but we take them as they come, rolling our eyes and nodding our heads until our authority figures grow tired of lecturing us. We then move on to make similar mistakes all over again. It's a vicious but very enlightening cycle.

Though I know my stubborn nature would probably have steered me away from taking any advice from anyone, I can't help but wonder how much heartache and embarrassment I could have avoided if I had only known then what I know now. And so, since I am NOT your mother or your father or anyone too mature to understand what goes on in the teen world these days, I'm hoping you might find some solace in my words. Because regardless of how you may feel most of the time, you are not going through this alone. And anyway, it helps to know someone else has made more ridiculous mistakes than you are making right now... and trust me, I have.

Growing Up Isn't Always Easy

There are so many decisions to make
at this time in your life
and so many changes with
family and friends.
Whether or not you know what
you want your career to be,
looking to the future can be overwhelming.
Work, school, or both take up
so much time and energy
that it seems like there's little left over
for fun and relaxation.
The future may not look as exciting
as it once did,
and it may even look a little
overwhelming at times.
The freedom that comes with adulthood
also comes with a lot of responsibility.
There are even more demands
on your time,
and people treat you like a child
in some ways,
but expect you to act like an adult
in others.

All you can do is your best.
Follow your heart
and use common sense.
Most of all, believe in yourself and
in your dreams.
You will likely have to make
some sacrifices
and work hard for a while,
but dreams are worth the effort.
The choices you make and the way
you live your life now
will determine what your future will be.
Every day is precious,
each moment unique.
Learn to enjoy and appreciate the beauty
and the people around you.
Make time to enjoy yourself,
but work hard, too.
You'll find that the present
and the future
can be all you could ever hope for.

♡ Barbara Cage

Be Yourself...

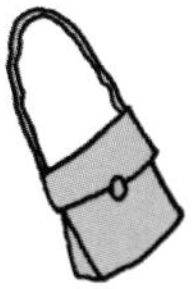

You've got to be real. Don't be a phony. Come on as yourself. The hardest thing in the world is to be something you're not. As you get closer and closer and closer to what you are, be that, and come on all the time that way. You'll find it's an easy way to live.

☆ Leo Buscaglia

If your friends laugh at what you wear,
laugh with them...
And wear it anyway.

☆ Judith Harlan

Develop autonomy, don't feel you have to be like the others; take your time about developing and all will turn out well.

☆ Jessie Bernard

Some people will be your friend
because of whom you know
Some people will be your friend
because of your position
Some people will be your friend
because of the way you look
Some people will be your friend
because of your possessions
But the only real friends
are the people who will be your friends
because they like you for how you are inside

☆ Susan Polis Schutz

Be yourself; the world will benefit from your talent and your humor. Search for people who love and appreciate you for who you are and who encourage you to improve. Don't be satisfied with less than all you can be, for you have greatness within you.

☆ Bill Cross

Tangerine Hair Dye...

The first lesson here is to steer clear of any hair-coloring product whose name originates from a food — specifically a fruit. "But it looks so pretty on the box," I pleaded with my mother. And of course, I followed that statement with one I have finally realized does not and never will work: "But Mom, everyone is doing it." "And if everyone were jumping off the Brooklyn Bridge, would you?" I had no answer for that one, and we both knew my fear of heights spoke for itself. But I was determined to be a redhead because the most popular girl in school said I had the perfect face for it (whatever that meant).

High school brought a million trends and fads that came on full blast, and though they all seemed as if they would last forever, each one faded out of existence, never to be revived again. Unfortunately, my fashionable new hair color didn't fade quite so easily, nor was it the ticket to popularity I had hoped it would be.

The word I would choose to describe myself in high school is "plain." I wanted more than anything to be part of the "in" crowd — the very stylish, trendy, nose-in-the-air, worshipped-by-boys crowd. I wanted to be one of those girls everyone deemed "perfect," and I would have done anything to fit in — to blend. I don't know what made me think the color "sunburst tangerine" would blend with anything but a fruit cocktail, but after I applied the dye to my blonde hair, it skipped right over the redhead stage and transformed me into an Easter egg — a bright orange Easter egg. As a result, my baseball cap became an essential part of my wardrobe that year... all for the sake of fitting in.

The moral of this story is not just to remember that the enticing color shown on the dye box is not the color your hair will turn out to be. It is also this: The most important thing to be while you're growing up is yourself. Unfortunately, growing up is filled with the stresses of fitting in and being popular. So many people succumb to conformity, changing their personality as many times as they change their underwear. There are a million cliques one can fall into: the popular kids, the rich kids, the brains, the jocks... the list goes on. It's easy, especially in junior high and high school, to fall into one of these groups in search of popularity. But you have to remember that ultimately, these groups don't choose you — you choose them.

Being popular is just a state of mind. Being confident and someone people want to be around are the true requirements of popularity. It has nothing to do with designer clothes or having the perfect body or whom you are dating. You should never try to change the person you are to fit someone else's mold. Be yourself and try to be friends with as many people as you can from all kinds of different groups. By opening yourself up to all kinds of people, you will experience so much more. People may be drawn to each other because they dress the same way or play the same sports, but that isn't what makes a friendship or a love relationship. It comes down to the kind of person and the kind of friend you are. You can't buy popularity in a box, and one day you will realize how much easier it is to just be you.

❀ ❀ ❀

When you are content to be simply yourself and don't compare or compete, everybody will respect you.

❀ *Lao-Tzu*

Men's Shoes...

You can't change people. What does that have to do with men's shoes, you ask? Okay, I have this fascination with shoes. If I don't like a guy's shoes, I usually won't date him. It is a ridiculous concept and I am aware of that, but I want to save you from doing something similar.

I dated this boy once who, overall, was a really great boyfriend... but his footwear left a little to be desired. For Christmas, I bought him a lovely pair of boots. He hated them. I loved them. I dropped hints constantly about what was in style, and after a while he grew tired of my antics and numerous attempts to improve him. He told me that if I wasn't satisfied with who he was, then we shouldn't be together. He was right. And here was a really great guy who I let walk right out of my life, wearing a pair of shoes I spent my entire paycheck on.

♡ ♡ ♡

The bottom line is that we are who we are, and we all want to be accepted for just that, not someone else's idea of who we could be.

♡ *Kimberly Kirberger*

This is about more than shoes. This is a life lesson that can be applied to every type of relationship you ever enter into. You can't mold people into something they are not. It just doesn't work. And you can't try to make someone perfect. No one is.

Throughout my life, I have tried to make people fit into an ideal that I created in my head. It's a waste of time because people are the way they are for a reason, and regardless of how you feel, they probably are happy that way. It's not fair to ask them to be someone they are not, just as it is not fair for a person to try to make you be someone you are not. Everyone is different and everyone has his or her own views and ideas about life and how to live it. This extends from a person's style to their morals and religious beliefs. Accept people for everything that they are; learn from people's differences and take what you can from your experiences with them. If someone makes you feel uncomfortable because of your differences (hopefully for a better reason than the style of your shoes), you may be better off without them.

Love Your Body...

The body is a compelling mystery, a constant focus of attention. At thirteen, I thought more about my acne than I did about God or world peace. At thirteen, many girls spend more time in front of a mirror than they do on their studies. Small flaws become obsessions. Bad hair can ruin a day. A broken fingernail can feel tragic.

Mary Pipher, Ph.D.

Your body is where you live. It is inseparable from who you are, and how you feel about it definitely affects how you feel about yourself.

Esther Drill, Heather McDonald, and Rebecca Odes

We are already perfect.
The world is already perfect.
We try to tamper with perfection,
and therein lies all of our problems.

Leo Buscaglia

Every girl feels a little insecure sometimes. Even me. So what can you do about it? Well, you can go and copy every new trend out there just to fit in with the crowd. But then you'll be spending a lot of money on some really tacky clothes. You can talk and act like the most popular girls in your school so they'll think you're cool, but that's lying to yourself as well as everyone else. Or you can hide in your room, hoping this phase will eventually pass. At some point you're going to realize, just as I did, that the only person you need to please is you.

❀ Britney Spears

Spend time shaping your LIFE,
not your body.

❀ Judith Harlan

Astringent Pads...

About a week before prom, a gross pimple erupted on my cheek. The end of the world? Possibly. My cabinets looked like the local pharmacy, and I tried every concoction possible (toothpaste, baking soda, lemon juice) to remove the pimple from my face. Two days before the big night, the light bulb popped on in my head (a sure sign to flip the switch off). I placed an astringent pad on my left cheek before bed and secured it into place with tape. I actually considered patenting this miracle cure at the time. I woke up to find a huge red circle branded on my face with the pimple resting happily in the center. I think I heard it laughing at me. Somehow, after a great deal of explaining and hundreds of dollars worth of makeup, I survived the prom. I even considered myself sane after my best friend informed me about her episode. She had to pass off her freak curling iron accident as an allergic reaction. Yes, she had tried to burn the pimple right off her forehead. We were only a little bit excessive.

Almost everyone in the world experiences some form of acne at one point in their lives. Unfortunately for most of us, it occurs in the adolescent stage, when looking good seems vital to survival. The key word to clear skin is "mild," which I, for the record, dumped from my vocabulary the moment it was uttered from my mother's mouth. "Use a mild cleanser," she said. "Pat dry, don't rub, use a mild lotion, and stop picking." I chose to ignore all of the above, and years later I'm realizing that sometimes Mom did know what she was talking about.

Over-washing can over-dry and cause more breakouts. This applies to topical medication as well. Healthy skin needs moisture, so stick with a mild cleanser and an oil-free moisturizer and give your face time to heal. If your acne is taking over your life, you may want to visit a dermatologist. The doctor will probably pick and probe at your face, prescribe some medication, and send you on your way. Don't expect miracles overnight. It takes time. And this is not the end of the world. People usually don't even notice the things we spend hours agonizing over. They do, however, notice burn marks, so steer clear of the curling iron.

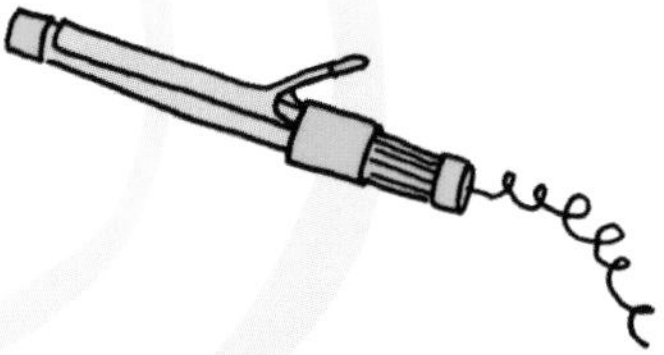

Diet Pills...

Don't take them. Basically, those tiny pills that promise to shed pounds before the sun sets are as ridiculous as standing on your head while consuming yogurt (yes, I tried this diet, too). Not only that, but they can be extremely dangerous. My best friend and I were in the mall when the pills caught my eye, but I was embarrassed to mention them to her (she being perfect, or so I thought at the time). I told her I'd meet up with her later and I made my purchase. After taking the pills, I was never hungry, so I rarely ate. I thought that was wonderful... until I found myself lying face down on the gym floor next to the treadmill I had fainted on. Try explaining that bruise to your mother. Or worse yet, to the hot guy who had to hoist me up off the floor. Not a very successful way to land a date.

☆ ☆ ☆

Women should stop thinking of themselves as products. Being products suggests powerlessness.... Women should learn to be their own judges of their adequacy rather than let other people or the media validate them.

☆ *Rosalyn M. Meadow, Ph.D., and Lillie Weiss, Ph.D.*

There are healthy ways to lose weight and keep it off. Taking what seems like the easy way out is not the way to go. It's so tempting with all the fad diets out there today. I know. I've tried everything from eating grapefruit before every meal to restricting myself to three weeks of cabbage soup to mixing hot dogs with ice cream (that last one was a doozy, but proves further what ridiculous things we will do to drop a few pounds). Fad diets don't work. I've spent more than half of my life on them. I always felt fat even when I wasn't. There will always be someone skinnier, someone more muscular, someone who looks better in the jeans you bought the day before, regardless of how many sit-ups you do or how many gallons of water you drink.

It is so important to set goals that are achievable. We are bombarded with images of people who are considered beautiful, but most of them are duct-taped and airbrushed to perfection. Trying to achieve such images can plummet you headfirst into an eating disorder before you even know it, and that is scary. Be fair to yourself and don't waste your time trying to be someone you can't be. I did, and I realize now how much time and energy I put into achieving an image that could only be achieved in magazines. Work out, drink some water, and eat your vegetables. You will be well on your way to a healthy body.

From the Heart of a Teenager...

Give us our little wishes, our own clothes, our harmless rebellions, the chance to make our own mistakes, to grow our special gardens. Tolerate our musings, as we learn and change our minds. Don't lead or we won't learn to walk alone, to see, or to speak our minds.

Listen before you judge us; we feel deeply and have reasons, too. Remember we must chase different dreams before we find what we best can do.

Trust our actions and our choices, however different from your own. Give us the courage to take chances, to know if we fall we are not alone. Have patience with our yearnings as we see our intentions through. Let us know that where we are coming from is a safe place to return to.

Allow us the freedom to be creative, the opportunity to be wrong. Teach us that we don't have to be perfect to belong. Give us our secret plans, our own music, our space to grow. Learn with us as we discover these things. When the time is right, let us go.

♡ Ashley Rice

Don't judge me by who I was or who I will be,
But by who I am right now.

Don't judge me by the clothes I wear on my body,
But by the expressions I wear on my face.

Don't judge me by how many friends I have,
But by the friends I choose.

Don't judge me by the color of my skin,
But by the color of my personality.

Don't judge me by how I speak,
But by what I listen to and what I hear.

Don't judge me by my eyes,
But by how my eyes look on the world.

In fact, don't judge me at all,
Because if you judge me,
Then you are only comparing me to you,
And I am not you.
I reflect you,
But I am not you.
If you stop judging me
And take the time to really see me,
Then you may find
That you love me for who I am.

♡ Jen Barnes, Age 19

New Kids on the Block Jacket...

I promised I'd wear it for the rest of my life and to my wedding if my parents would let me buy it. It was finally put to rest a few years ago in the back of an old closet and will remain there... probably forever.

I was obsessed with the band and spent every penny I ever made on New Kids on the Block souvenirs. My parents watched as every cent of allowance and every babysitting dollar was exchanged for posters, clothing, pins, and books covered with the faces of Jon, Joey, Donnie, Danny, and Jordan, my idols. At the time, I wouldn't have it any other way. Now, having struggled through college counting change for food and saving up to pay back loans, I wish someone would've stopped me.

The part of us that is eternal has no image. The part of us that lasts is pure spirit. The things in our heart, not the clothes on our body, are the real us.

Bonnie M. Parsley

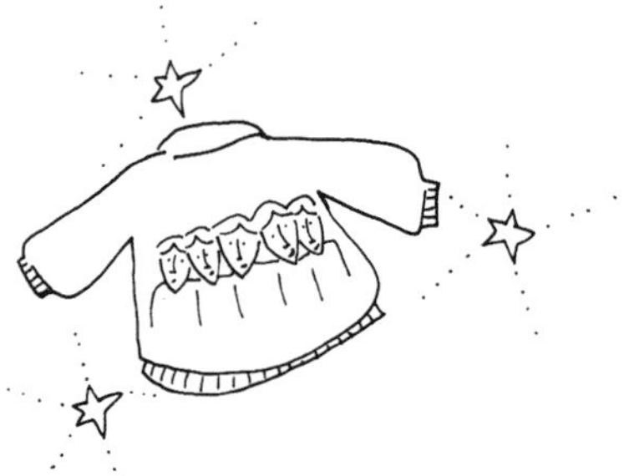

I've learned now, a little late, to think through every purchase I make. Fads come and go quicker than we can get our hands on them and before we know it, the next style hits the store windows, replacing the one we just purchased.

It's so important to save money, especially during these teen years. There is so much you're going to want to do, to see, and to experience, and having extra money saved makes it so much easier. I could plan a tropical vacation or buy an entire new wardrobe for the amount of money I spent on NKOTB gear. Before making a purchase, decide how long the item is going to last you. Ask yourself if you are buying it because you really like it or because someone else has it or likes it. And remember: chances are you **will not** wear it forever, though it may at some point make a good Halloween costume.

Being a Friend...

True friendship is a plant of slow growth, and must undergo and withstand the shocks of adversity before it is entitled to the appellation.

♡ George Washington

Two are better than one, because they have a good reward for their labor. For if they fall, one will lift up his companion. But woe to him who is alone when he falls, for he has no one to help him up.... Though one may be overpowered by another, two can withstand him. And a threefold cord is not quickly broken.

♡ Ecclesiastes 4:9-10, 12 (NKJV)

It is not so much our friends' help that helps us as the confident knowledge that they will help us.

♡ Epicurus

The glory of friendship is not the outstretched hand, nor the kindly smile, nor the joy of companionship; it is the spiritual inspiration that comes to one when he discovers that someone else believes in him and is willing to trust him.

♡ Ralph Waldo Emerson

Friendship is more than perfect moments
sweet memories and happy bouts of laughter
It finds us in our lowest times
and picks us up to begin again
Friendship is the strength
when we are too weak to progress
It is our heart when we are too numb to feel
Friendship brings us to see ourselves
for what we truly are
for what we someday can be
Friendship is our hope, our comfort
and sometimes the truth we'd rather not hear
It is the foundation that keeps us whole
that holds our hand as well as our heart
It is the promise of forever

♡ Deana Marino

Courage...

You are going to need it if your friend plummets into the black hole of experimentation and you need to pick up the pieces. Adolescence is a time when we all claim the need to find ourselves and to fit in. And no one ever said it was going to be easy, but for some people it becomes a harder task than for others.

My best friend grew up while the rest of us were just entering puberty. We learned to accept her wildness and even liked it at times, but as we grew older and our horizons were broadened, things weren't so funny anymore. We watched one of our best friends fall headfirst into a drug addiction. At first I wanted to be there for her. I would leave my back door open so that she could stumble into my house and have a place to stay on the nights when she was too messed up to go home. I felt I was being a good friend by keeping her off the streets. Those nights became more frequent and I grew more and more afraid of what was to come. One night I stared at my door for hours and finally turned the lock and went to bed. The police found her on a bench sometime in the night and she was arrested. I knew what I had done may have cost me her friendship, but it was better than losing her completely. She eventually got her act together and though we will never be as close as we once were, I know that in her heart she is thankful.

Friendship is more than just the fun times. It can be painful and it can be hard. Not all situations are the same, and there are different ways of dealing with different people. Don't confront a lone person as a group, because that will make the person feel isolated and ganged up on. Talking to them one-on-one is best, but if you know it will just anger them, don't waste your time; it could make matters worse.

The decision to tell someone, like a parent, sibling, or teacher, is a big one. If you have a group of friends who all know the situation, you should address the problem together. This is a tough situation to deal with on your own, and you have to realize that you, alone, do not have the power to end a friend's addiction. You need help.

It is a long and hard process that may jeopardize your relationship, but you must remember that you are being the best friend you can possibly be under the circumstances. It may be the hardest choice you will ever have to make, but making the right one can save a life. Remember that.

Myself

I have to live with myself, and so
I want to be fit for myself to know;
I want to be able as days go by
Always to look myself straight in the eye;
I don't want to stand with the setting sun
And hate myself for the things I've done.

I don't want to keep on a closet shelf
A lot of secrets about myself,
And fool myself as I come and go
Into thinking that nobody else will know
The kind of person I really am;
I don't want to dress myself up in sham.

I want to go out with my head erect,
I want to deserve all people's respect;
But here in the struggle for fame and pelf,
I want to be able to like myself.
I don't want to think as I come and go
That I'm bluster and bluff and empty show.

I never can hide myself from me,
I see what others may never see,
I know what others may never know,
I never can fool myself — and so,
Whatever happens, I want to be
Self-respecting and conscience free.

☆ Edgar A. Guest

Virginity...

There are a million reasons why you should wait... because you can't take it back... because you thought he'd love you... because it doesn't seem like a big deal at the time... because — well, just because. It is mental. It is about your mind and your heart and sharing a piece of yourself with someone else. It is physical. It is about your body and not only how you feel physically, but the consequences your physical self could possibly endure... the pregnancy, the diseases... you've heard it all before. And we've all said, "It won't happen to me." Quite famous lines that go hand in hand with the other fallacy: "He won't love me if I don't." It **can** happen to you and if he doesn't love you now, chances are, he **won't** love you after.

I couldn't even tell you the day of the week I decided to share myself with him, but I can remember perfectly the look on my best friend's face a month later as we waited the longest three minutes of my life for pink or blue to appear on that test. It kills me that that day will remain more vivid than any sexual experience I'll ever have. The truth is, I wasn't ready to deal with the consequences, with what would've happened if that test had been positive, and so, though it's hard to admit, I wasn't ready to be having sex.

No one can tell you if you're ready to have sex. Your parents will say you're not ready until you turn 55; your best friend will say she was ready so you're probably ready; your boyfriend... well, you know he thinks you're ready. But no one truly knows what's going on inside your mind, your heart, and your body — except you. It's not just about the act, it's about the million things that come after. The scariest part is that you can't take it back. And regardless of how right it may feel in the moment, you need to decide if it will be worth it when that moment passes and you plunge back into reality.

There is so much pressure, but it doesn't matter if everyone's doing it or if no one is doing it at all. What matters is how you feel inside and how you'll feel tomorrow and how you'll feel five years down the line looking back. It's not about your boyfriend or your parents or your best friend; it's about you. Don't ever forget that.

✿ ✿ ✿

I want you to know the truth of two people so close and caring that there seems to be no distance. I want you to know the joy of tears rolling down your cheeks from the beauty you have shared. But most of all, I want you to be able to look in the eyes of the [person] in your arms and say, "I love you," with a pure heart. If you can, you are truly making love. If you can't, you are just having sex. And the distance between the two is the distance between the earth and the heavens.

✿ *Kent Nerburn*

Pleasing Your Parents

I woke up this morning
At quarter past seven.
I kicked up the covers
And stuck out my toe.
And ever since then
(That's a quarter past seven)
They haven't said anything
Other than "no."
They haven't said anything
Other than "Please, dear,
Don't do what you're doing,"
Or "Lower your voice."
Whatever I've done
And however I've chosen,
I've done the wrong thing
And I've made the wrong choice.
I didn't wash well
And I didn't say thank you.
I didn't shake hands
And I didn't say please.
I didn't say sorry
When passing the candy.
I banged the box into
Miss Witelson's knees.

I didn't say sorry.
I didn't stand straighter.
I didn't speak louder
When asked what I'd said.
Well, I said
That tomorrow
At quarter past seven
They can
Come in and get me.
I'm Staying In Bed.

♡ Karla Kuskin

Quarter in Your Pocket...

If I had one now for every time my mother questioned if I had one before leaving the house, I'd be a millionaire. I rolled my eyes each time she said it. Come to think of it, I rolled my eyes each time she said almost anything. She insisted on my having the quarter so that if I ever found myself in a situation where I felt the need, I could call home. In this age of cell phones, it may not seem as significant, but batteries die, pocketbooks get misplaced, and phones get lost. It is inevitable. A few of those instances took place in my life, ranging from locked keys in running cars to friends who had a little too much to drink. And though I wouldn't admit it then, that quarter was a lifesaver at times.

One of those times occurred at a party in a big field under a New York City overpass (one of our usual hangouts). Things got a bit crazy and our designated driver was no longer capable of being designated — or of doing much else, now that I think about it. I should've been home a half-hour earlier, and though I feared my parents' wrath, I had no choice but to call home. Instead of taking the usual route of blaming a lost cab driver or an alien invasion, I began with the truth. There was no yelling or crying or any of the other stuff that would usually go hand in hand with these situations. My parents understood. They respected me for making a mature decision and trusted me more than ever.

Believe it or not, your parents are people, too, and though many times their ideas may seem ancient or their advice might seem corny, they were once young and they do understand... if you give them the chance. Communication is a huge part of growing up happy in your home. Many of the things parents do that annoy you, such as setting curfews, are done not because they don't trust you, but because they are afraid of other people or things beyond their control. If you talk things out with your parents and explain that you are responsible and should be trusted because of the way they brought you up, they may step back and realize that you just might be right.

You should feel free to use that quarter if you are ever put in a situation that you know is dangerous or makes you feel uncomfortable. Know that no matter how much trouble you think you may be in, it is far better to call home than to put yourself in a situation that can hurt you. It is a trust thing, and if parents know that they can trust your judgment and your decisions, then life will be a lot easier for everyone. There will always be things that you want to do that they don't want you to do. That is unavoidable, but for the most part, being honest and feeling comfortable talking with your parents can make for less heartache and more independence.

When Somebody Dies...

a cloud turns into an angel
and flies up to tell God
to put another flower on a pillow.
A bird gives the message back
to the world
and sings a silent prayer
that makes the rain cry.
People disappear, but they never
really go away.
The spirits up there
put the sun to bed,
wake up the grass,
and spin the Earth in dizzy circles.
Sometimes you can see them
dancing in a cloud during the daytime
when they're supposed to be sleeping.
They paint the rainbows
and also the sunsets
and make waves splash
and tug at the tide.
They toss shooting stars
and listen to wishes.
And when they sing wind-songs,
they whisper to us,
"Don't miss me too much.
The view is nice,
and I'm doing just fine."

Ashley Rice

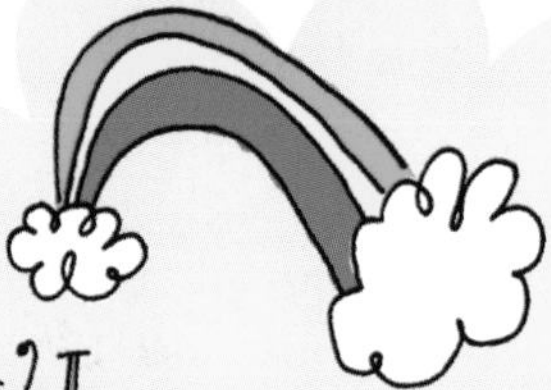

Finding Strength

There are times in every life
when we feel hurt or alone.
But I believe that these times
when we feel lost
and all around us seems
to be falling apart
are really bridges of growth.
We struggle and try to recapture
the security of what was,
but almost in spite of ourselves
we emerge on the other side
with a new understanding,
a new awareness,
a new strength.
It is almost as though
we must go through the pain
and the struggle
in order to grow
and reach new heights.

Sue Mitchell

Sealed Letter...

My grandpa died when I was away at college. The phone call hit me like a ton of bricks. These things are so hard because you have no control over them and no say in them. It makes you angry and sad and confused and regretful and a million other things that eat you up inside, but when you look out your window, the world steadily goes on as if nothing has changed. That's what got me the most. I remember the drive home and how the radio broadcaster's voice made me cringe as I realized that the world was still going about its business when all I wanted was for it to stop and grieve with me.

I was angry with my family because they were given the chance to say goodbye and I wasn't. I knew I had to find closure somehow, so I wrote the longest letter I have ever written. I spilled every ounce of my feelings onto that paper and kept on writing until my hand hurt. I shared everything with my grandfather in that letter, things I wished I would've said years ago, things about my future that I wanted him to experience with me, and everything in between. I sealed the envelope and carried it with me through all the services that weekend.

Writing that letter cleared my mind. It brought me a form of comfort that nothing else could have provided. In my heart, I believe my grandpa heard my words, and that has helped me to get on with my life. We are sad when someone dies, but more than that, we are angry, and it's so much harder because the person we are angry with is not around to help us come to any resolutions. For me, writing that letter was my resolution, my apology for everything I had ever done wrong, and my happiness for all that we had shared together.

Losing someone we love hurts — there is no way around that. But keeping all your emotions cooped up inside is not healthy. Talk to someone, write a letter, or talk out loud to yourself or to the person who has passed away. Just because the person is no longer present physically doesn't mean you can't still speak to them and share with them the many things on your mind. When I visit my grandpa's grave, I tell him everything that is going on in my life. I still get sad that he is not around to share things with me, but I feel like he is with me inside and remains, in many ways, a part of my life.

♡ ♡ ♡

Give sorrow words.... The grief that does not speak, whispers the o'erfraught heart, and bids it break.

♡ *William Shakespeare*

Sorry Note...

My uncle was a huge part of my life growing up. Every childhood memory I have is colored with his presence, but as with many people, certain circumstances caused him to fade out of my life. I eventually came to understand that an argument between him and my father had pushed him away, but at the time, I believed it was somehow my fault, that for some reason he didn't want to spend time with me. I wrote an angry letter that I'm sure must have hurt him just as much as I was hurting at the time. I didn't see him for years. The one time I did, he made every effort to make amends; in my stubbornness, I ignored each and every one.

I was away at college a few years later when my mother called to tell me my uncle had died of a sudden heart attack. I remember first thinking I didn't care, but then it hit me how much I really did love him and how angry I was with myself for wasting so many of my years holding a grudge. I saw his wife at the funeral and she told me that he cared about me very much. All I wanted was to be able to tell him that I cared, too, but I hadn't been given the chance. Actually, I had been given many chances. I just chose not to take them, and now I will never be able to get that time back or to say that I'm sorry... and I am.

Throughout life, people will hurt you. Many times they will be the people who are closest to you — friends, family, lovers. Forgiveness is tough, but life is too short to hold grudges. It seems so much easier to be angry at a person or to keep feelings inside and continue on as if nothing has happened. Either way, you are hurting and your relationship is going to be affected somehow.

Not everyone is good at confronting their feelings. Sometimes it may be easier to write a letter instead of talking. But whichever way you choose to deal with how you are feeling, make sure you deal with it. People don't communicate enough. They tell others how they feel, but they don't tell the people who are directly involved. Part of being mature enough to enter into relationships is having the ability to be open and honest. People mess up; that is part of life. You can accept that and work on bettering your relationships or you can hold grudges and isolate yourself from people you care about. When you look back, as I do now, you will wish you would've chosen the first.

☆ ☆ ☆

Life appears to me too short to be spent in nursing animosity, or registering wrongs.

☆ *Charlotte Brontë*

After a While

After a while you learn
the subtle difference between
holding a hand and chaining a soul
and you learn
that love doesn't mean leaning
and company doesn't always mean security.
And you begin to learn
that kisses aren't contracts
and presents aren't promises
and you begin to accept your defeats
with your head up and your eyes ahead
with the grace of a woman,
not the grief of a child
and you learn
to build all your roads on today
because tomorrow's ground is
too uncertain for plans
and futures have a way of falling down
in mid-flight.

After a while you learn
that even sunshine burns
if you get too much
so you plant your own garden
and decorate your own soul
instead of waiting for someone
to bring you flowers.
And you learn that you really can endure
you really are strong
you really do have worth
and you learn
and you learn
with every goodbye, you learn.

♡ Veronica A. Shoffstall

Ballpoint Pen...

I am quite embarrassed at some of the things I did out of what seemed at the time to constitute love, and I can only hope that none of you have exhibited this kind of obsessive behavior. When we fall for a boy, especially one who seems out of our reach, some of us tend to get a little crazy. (Yes, I'm raising my hand.) I had a habit of raising guys up onto pedestals and doing everything but bowing down to them. After taping photographs to my walls, writing my name with his last name a million times, and wearing T-shirts that advertised his favorite band, I can honestly say that no guy is that amazing, or that untouchable.

A guy may want you to think he is perfect, but he knows he's not. Don't be fooled. I was. In high school, I was so crazy about this one guy. He was one year older and perfect, or so I thought. We took the same bus home from school and one day he was writing something on a piece of paper. He dropped his pen. I picked it up. I brought it home and swore I'd write with it for the rest of my life. That's not the bad part. He knew. I don't know how, but when he and his friends threw pens at me out of the bus window one afternoon, I thought my life was over.

✿ ✿ ✿

You feel butterflies in your stomach, your head throbs and you can't for the life of you figure out why.

✿ *Dee Snider*

The moral of this story is not only NOT to collect souvenirs, but also for you to understand the importance of having confidence in yourself. See, about a year later, after the pen incident subsided and I had seen my crush spotted with enough chicken pox to know he wasn't so perfect, he and I began to date. I finally got up the courage to talk to him and found out he was just a normal guy. His quietness, which I once took for coolness, was really shyness, and little by little I realized he was just as nervous as I was. This is the case with most boys, but most girls never have enough confidence to make themselves noticed.

One thing I've always had to work on is confidence. I was so afraid of rejection. Why would someone like that be interested in someone like me? This is a question that haunts so many of us and the answer is: because you have a lot more to offer than you think you do and if you don't give it a chance, you will never know. A boy senses confidence. In most cases, boys do not want to date girls who idolize them. That is a hard thing to live up to. They want to date girls they can pal around and be themselves with. Why waste your time pasting his face to your wall when you can talk to him in person? I know it's not easy (I still have trouble with this one sometimes), but get to know him, let him see that you're a pretty cool person, and in the worst-case scenario, you will make a new friend.

Love Letter...

It all seems so wonderful at the time. Why wouldn't it be... telling your sweetheart how happy he makes you and how much you love being with him... adding in some lyrics from a popular song and maybe even a poem. Blah, blah, blah...

Save yourself while you can. Don't write anything you wouldn't want read over a PA speaker or written in the sky. I am a writer. I love to write. It is easier for me to put my feelings on paper than to speak them out loud. It always has been. So I wrote a letter to this boy I liked. I used pretty paper (went through almost a whole pad before I got every word right) and wrote in my best penmanship in blue ink, because blue was his favorite color. I included a song by Debbie Gibson. (Yes, she used to be cool.) I wrote out every word. I was IN LOVE. It was great until a bunch of other guys gathered in the corner of the schoolyard to read just how in love I really was. They called me Debbie Gibson for the rest of the year. Needless to say, the boy I thought I was so in love with and I are no longer an item.

Remember, once things are written down, it is very difficult to take them back. It's hard to think about the future when your relationship is going really well, but there is always the chance that this will not last forever. The love letter you write now is a keepsake that will live on and that can be pulled out, referred to, or read out loud at any time. So if you do write a letter, choose your words wisely.

It isn't a bad thing to share your feelings with someone. Writing little notes or even sending a greeting card can be nice gestures to let someone know how you feel. But there are limits, and sometimes it's better to keep a boy guessing. Though it's nice to share your feelings, professing your love makes your relationship too easy. Boys like a challenge. If you tell them over and over again how perfect they are, they will begin to believe you. They may even thank you for boosting their self-esteem as they walk out the door to see how other girls feel about them. Don't shower a guy with gifts or make him the center of your world. Make him believe that he is lucky to be dating you, not the other way around. (It's true, you know.) Play it cool and don't try too hard.

Breaking Up Is Hard to Do...

Take the time to be alone,
so you can know just how terrific
your own company can be.
Remember that being alone
doesn't always mean being lonely;
it can be a beautiful experience
of finding your creativity,
your heartfelt feelings,
and the calm and quiet peace deep inside you.

Jacqueline Schiff

Some of the most beautiful, talented, and wonderful women in the world have failed to win the men they wanted so you would be in good company. If you succeed, fine; if you don't, well just chalk it up to experience.

Jessie Bernard

You know you're not the only one
Who has a lot to overcome
And when the time has come then you move on
'Cause you've been crying for too long
Sometimes life is so unkind
But change is never a waste of time

Alanis Morissette, Leslie Howe, and Serge Cote

There will be times
when love seems lost
and hate conquers reason.

There will be moments
when trust leads to heartbreak
and doubts rule your thoughts.

There will be days
when all hope seems deceiving,
when serenity succumbs to chaos,
when it hurts even to breathe.

I wish for you a thousand smiles
to smooth your feelings when torn apart.
I wish for you a blanket of warmth
to give you peace and ease your sleep.
I wish for you a bouquet of kindness
for you to nurture a new beginning.

❀ Leeza Azraen, Age 19

Headband...

As much as a guy might like you to think he is your other half, he's not. He is an accessory to your life, like a pair of earrings or a headband. You can get on without him, I promise. Breakups hurt. There is no way around it. But regardless of how much your heart hurts, it is not the end of the world. Chances are, unless you are lucky enough to find the guy of your dreams at age twelve, your life will be filled with numerous breakups.

My first real breakup caught me off-guard, and I wasn't prepared to deal with how painful it was going to be. My boyfriend broke up with me over the phone for no real reason. He just needed some "space." (Get used to that one; they all use it.) I locked myself in my room and refused to talk to anyone. I didn't think it was worth living without him (an absolutely insane thought we all feel during one breakup or another). When I finally stopped feeling sorry for myself and unlocked my bedroom door to see the light of day, I devoted countless hours to getting him back. I wrote letters, I had friends talk to him, I even drove by his house a million times a day to see how he was surviving without me ("How could he be?" was my thought). Then I moved on to the make-him-jealous phase, trying to date people he knew so he could see what he was missing. Needless to say, I was borderline crazy, and unfortunately for me, this was not a turn-on for him.

I realize now how ridiculous I made myself look and how insane it was to believe that I couldn't survive without him. The mistakes I made after the breakup began while we were dating. I made him the center of my world and so, of course, when he wasn't part of it anymore I felt torn apart.

A boyfriend should complement you and make you a better person, not become your other half. You have to uphold your identity in a relationship and have your own life outside of each other. This is very important to having a healthy relationship and to surviving a breakup. You cannot be afraid of being alone. I will admit to being the first person who falls victim to this fear. It is nice to have a boyfriend to do things with and to share a part of your life with, but you must have a foundation if he should happen not to be there anymore.

Breakups are hard regardless. We all need our sob time, our container-of-ice-cream time, and our curl-into-bed-and-feel-sorry-for-ourselves time. But we need to pick ourselves up, sometimes with help from our friends or families, and get back out in the world. Realize the world doesn't stop because you are hurting, and it will continue to go on whether you choose to join it or not. Do the things you always enjoyed doing, with or without a boyfriend. Watch movies, read books, go walking, exercise, go to the mall, go fishing. (There are plenty of fish in the sea, you know.)

Valentine's Day...

This was the day I realized my boyfriend had consumed every waking moment of my life, and that I had somehow pushed away my friends to what seemed like the other side of the world. I didn't even realize I had done it. I was at a point in my life where I was so preoccupied with my love life that nothing else seemed to matter, and I was shocked to find out that it was the things I had given little thought to that really did matter the most.

In college, my roommates (also my best friends) planned a Valentine's Day party. I already had plans with my boyfriend and was so angry that they wouldn't change the date so that I could attend. I was more than angry; I was hurt. What I didn't realize was that they were hurt, too. I wasn't around much and though they weren't happy about it, life went on without me. I wasn't there to confide in when any of them had problems, and I wasn't there to hear about the exciting things that went on in their lives. I had drifted so far away from them that even if I were at the Valentine's party, I probably would've spent the entire night with my boyfriend, as I had done so many nights before. It was impossible to make up for lost time, and having been out of the loop for so long, it was extremely difficult to find my way back.

That old saying, "Boyfriends come and go, but friends last forever" — well, just in case you weren't sure... it's true. The friendships you make will carry you through life — through crises and good times and breakups and losses. They will make you strong and ease your pain when you are weak. There will always be times when life gets hectic and there's not enough time to balance everything at once. This happens to everyone. But don't lose touch. Let a friend know what's going on in your life and that when things are back to normal, you'll be around again.

Loyalty is a huge part of friendship. When other activities and people begin to take up your time, it is important not to forget about the people who have always been there for you. There are things that friendship can provide that love relationships cannot, and though you may not realize it, these are the things you'll miss the most if you don't make time for them now. Looking back on the years I spent with my boyfriend, little bonding experiences are the things I missed — things like staying up late talking or seeing a good movie or going shopping. And though I am very close with my girlfriends now, I can never get that time back. Friendship is the most wonderful thing in the world. Don't ever forget that.

Have the Will to Win...

You can't coach heart,
You can never coach desire;
They must always come from within.
Rules may be learned, and skills developed,
But you cannot be taught the will to win.
You must reach a little deeper
To bring out your best;
You must be your own motivation.
Keep going, never quit, you have to have a reason,
You are your own strength, your own inspiration.

♡ Melissa Underwood, Age 15

Believe in whatever you think is worth believing in, and never stop until you feel you have done all that you can to secure your dreams.

♡ T. L. Nash

Get to know yourself
Find out who you are
Choose your goals carefully
Be honest with yourself
But don't think about yourself so much
that you analyze every word and action
Don't become preoccupied with yourself
Find many interests and pursue them
Find out what is important to you
Find out what you are good at
Don't be afraid to make mistakes
Work hard to achieve successes
When things are not going right
don't give up — just try harder

♡ Susan Polis Schutz

Our greatest glory consists not in never falling,
But in rising every time we fall.

♡ Confucius

Sidewalk...

If it hadn't been there, I would've gotten my license the first time... and the second time. It seems like when you're behind the wheel with your mom, friend, driving instructor, et cetera, everything goes as smooth as butter. But the minute you step into the car for the actual driving test, you lose control. It's all about composure and sheer confidence — two things I left at home the morning of my road test. I was shaking so badly I could barely hold the steering wheel. It seemed like a matter of life and death. And apparently, hitting the curb during a parallel parking job is just that — a matter of death. I told the instructor that I hardly tapped it and he said that if a person were standing on the curb, I would've killed him. "If" is the key word, but there were no buts about this one. Trust me, I tried.

The second time was basically a bad rerun of the first time. After once again slamming my back tire against the concrete, I tried to explain that my uncle was a driver's education teacher (as if that should excuse me). I was told with a sarcastic smirk to go get myself free lessons. I did eventually pass my road test about a month later, after hours and hours of practicing wedging my car between two cones my parents set up in front of our home. The third time was a charm.

If only I could've been calm the first time I took the test, I would've parked that car with no questions asked. It is not a life or death matter (unless you actually do hop a curb where ten people are waiting for a bus), and it is not the end of the world if you don't pass. I'm living proof that there always is a next time.

If you practice hard enough and keep your calm the day of the test, there is a good chance you can walk away with a driver's license the first time around. The instructor may seem intimidating, but one day, a long time ago, he or she was sitting in that same driver's seat going through the exact same motions. They are not out to get you. Have confidence in yourself and remember all the things you have learned, like making complete stops and counting to three at the stop signs. If it were that impossible, there would be a lot more people in the world riding bikes. Watch out for that curb, and you'll be driving around before you know it.

❀ ❀ ❀

Loosen up.... To desire success is a splendid thing but to pursue success too tensely is to make certain of missing it.

❀ *Emmet Fox*

No One Said It Was Easy...

Life is difficult. This is a great truth, one of the greatest truths. It is a great truth because once we truly see this truth, we transcend it. Once we truly know that life is difficult — once we truly understand and accept it — then life is no longer difficult. Because once it is accepted, the fact that life is difficult no longer matters.

☆ M. Scott Peck, M.D.

When you get into a tight place and everything goes against you, till it seems as though you could not hang on a minute longer, never give up then, for that is just the place and time that the tide will turn.

☆ Harriet Beecher Stowe

...Junior high is not all of life. There are other places — the mountains and beaches, the family cabin on the lake or the neighborhood clubhouse. There are other people — neighbors, relatives, family friends, old people and babies. And there are other times. [You] will not always be trapped in teenagehood; people do grow up.

☆ Mary Pipher, Ph.D.

Sometimes...

When we think too much about ourselves
We get exhausted and depressed
When we think too much about others
We get tired and stressed
When we expect too much in life
We think no one cares

So...

Feel good about what you have
Enjoy the good company around you

And...

Smell the roses while passing by
Achieve your goals and aim high
Search the deepest truth in your heart
Treasure the precious company while being apart
Take care of the heart and soul
True happiness is the ultimate goal
Give smiles to frowning faces
Heal up the bruises
Hope for the best
And cope with the rest

☆ Kurin Seventh

Chamomile Tea...

When I think back on high school, the first thing that comes to mind is a stomachache; the second is chamomile tea. I spent so much time in the nurse's office that I had to buy her a gift when I graduated. It was because I was way too high-strung and stressed-out about nothing. Without knowing it, I was a very nervous person, so it made sense when my doctor said that I had a nervous stomach. A big exam, a confrontation with a teacher, a party: all these kinds of circumstances landed me in the nurse's office. No one could figure it out.

After being poked and prodded, drinking gallons of clear fluid, and having tubes stuck in places they shouldn't be stuck, my problems were linked to my thoughts — both conscious and subconscious. Just thinking on a Thursday about a date I had on Friday gave me a stomachache. The smell of my perfume before leaving for a party gave me a stomachache. It was bizarre. Eventually, I learned how to talk my way through the pain and to make myself believe the things that made me nervous weren't a big deal at all.

The thing is, so much of how we feel is controlled by our thoughts. Sometimes we don't even know we are thinking about anything at all. Talking ourselves through fear, sadness, anger, or anxiety can relieve a huge amount of the unnecessary stress we hold on our shoulders every day. It may also help to talk things out with others or to keep a journal. Clearing your mind and putting your thoughts in perspective eliminates stress, and we certainly don't need any additional stress in our lives.

Making "to do" lists can help in budgeting your time so that you don't feel like you are cramming a million things into a short period of time. The night before a big test, my mother would always say, "If you don't know it by now, you won't know it, and it's not the end of the world." She was right. We put way too much pressure on ourselves sometimes. We need to enjoy life more and not take everything so seriously. Yes, school is important, but it's not everything, and chances are you will perform better — not only in school, but in life — if you don't stress out so much.

Almost all the wisdom of the world agrees: worrying doesn't really accomplish anything. All it does is get in the way of moving on and making the day brighter.

Douglas Pagels

Learn as Much as You Can...

Think, read, study diligently day by day, and the severest tests of your knowledge shall find you prepared and confident. Do not lose sleep over the prospect of examinations, or fret above the printed page until you cannot read its lessons clear.... Face your deficiencies and acknowledge them; but do not let them master you. Let them teach you patience, sweetness, insight.

♡ Helen Keller

The essence of education is not to stuff you with facts but to help you to discover your uniqueness, to teach you how to develop it, and then to show you how to give it away.

Learning is the greatest joy. To learn something is fantastic because every time you learn something you become something new.

♡ Leo Buscaglia

Education is not given for the purpose of earning a living; it's learning what to do with a living after you've earned it.

♡ Abraham Lincoln

Teachers open the door, but you must enter by yourself.

♡ Chinese Proverb

Adults are books.... The trick is to read these old books like you read your favorite novels. Listen to the stories and heed the warnings. Find the wisdom stored in these old pages. Then become the author of your own book, one that shapes your world according to *your* own vision.

♡ Judith Harlan

General Steward...

I thought he freed the slaves until I was in high school, and to this day I still have no idea what role he played in American history. Yet somehow I managed to graduate from grade school with my name on the "top banana list." It haunts me now, years later, when things that are common knowledge to most people are mind-boggling to me. And though I blame my not-so-ingenious teacher, I have to blame myself as well, for sitting back and taking the ride without questioning why I hadn't learned the state capitals, but I could recite every story from the entire Bible backwards.

My Social Studies teacher doubled as my religion teacher. She lived, breathed, and loved religion, so in turn, we were supposed to do the same. Sixth period Social Studies turned into a prayer service at least once a week, and the rest of the days blend together in my head as one religious experience after the next. We watched a ton of movies and wrote in our journals, which basically constituted passing notes to each other and playing tic-tac-toe. Our class was given A's in History across the board, so no one ever thought to question it. That was until my mother and I were having a stimulating conversation about slavery, and I proceeded to tell her what a nice man General Steward was for freeing the slaves. She, having no clue who this man even was, plunged me directly into summer school history classes and rallied the rest of the parents against the religious lady who liked to call herself a teacher. Needless to say, history will never be my strong point.

Though at the time I would have told you I was learning too much, when I look back on my education, I wish I would have learned more. I don't mean I wish I had studied harder, I mean I wish I had taken advantage of the resources around me: the people, the environment, and the activities. Though I swore hatred for them at 4 a.m. the night before a paper was due or when I received a "C" when I thought it was going to be an "A," I realize now how intelligent my teachers really were and how much more I could have absorbed from them.

Don't look at your teachers as enemies, but try to develop a relationship with them so you feel comfortable asking questions and talking about things. This will not be the case with all the teachers you encounter, but try to get close with as many as you can. They are not in your life just to teach you what is in your textbook; they can provide guidance, advice, and open your mind to so much if you give them the chance. Education is not just about the grades. It's about the experience and what you take from it. Be busy as much as you can. Join clubs and activities. It will feel good to know you did something and to look back on your school years and know you squeezed out every last drop.

Math Test...

We can rationalize it in our heads as guidance or help or even a wandering eye, but cheating is just that: it's cheating, no matter how much you try to justify it. If you have any doubt in your head at any time, even the smallest inkling of guilt creeping up from the pit of your stomach, then chances are you are doing something you shouldn't be doing.

I learned the hard way. We were taking an in-class math exam and for one part, we could work together with a partner. I had been paired up with the most popular girl in my class and she asked to check my answers with her own. I guess inside I knew this was cheating, but she was so popular and she did say check her answers, not copy, so why not? I remember sweating bullets. I remember the lump in my throat. And worst of all, I remember the sound of the red pen scratching an "F" at the top of both our papers. I had to go home and face my parents, have them sign the F-paper, and bring it back the next day. It was awful.

The thing is, you know when something doesn't feel right. You can either swallow down that funny feeling and continue on, or you can take the time to do your own work and not risk getting in trouble. Cheating seems so easy sometimes, but teachers are a lot smarter than you think. They have read millions of books and papers and can recognize work that doesn't belong to you. You may save some time, but is it really worth the risk of failing or having people not be able to trust you? If you do get caught, people will question whether the rest of the work you have done is your own, and it is very hard to gain back trust once it is lost.

There were so many times when it would've been so much easier to copy an essay out of a book or off the Internet instead of staying up all night to write a huge paper, but getting a good grade and knowing I worked hard was such an amazing feeling. It's nice to be able to pat yourself on the back once in a while and know that whatever grade you earn is yours, regardless of what it is.

Rise Above Adversity...

No one can make you feel inferior without your consent.

❀ Eleanor Roosevelt

Just because I didn't fit into their mold didn't mean I wasn't somebody. Besides, *they didn't even know me.* I was somebody, and it was at sixteen that for the first time I said it to myself and believed it. I liked the feeling, too. Whether or not others believed it didn't matter, as long as I did.

❀ Dee Snider

Keep away from people who try to belittle your ambitions. Small people always do that, but the really great make you feel that you, too, can become great.

❀ Mark Twain

You have to say what you feel
if you want people to know what is on your mind.
You have to search for what you want
and not regret what you don't find.
When you are sad, you have to bite your lip
and dry the tears from your eyes.
When you are all alone and lost,
you have to find your own way to make it home.
When no one else will listen to you
or they do not understand,
don't worry — you'll survive without a helping hand.
You have to look up to the sky
when you are feeling low,
and when you think the sadness will not end,
soon it will go.
Always remember life is a challenge,
and the more you learn,
the more you will be glad to know.

Jodi Lynn, Age 19

Two Points...

My third grade teacher always asked where those two points had gone. It didn't matter how well I did. On a test score of 98, I was asked where the other two points had gone. I hated how I felt inside, like I could never do well enough. School always seemed like a competition, and instead of being satisfied when I knew I had done my best, I always felt disappointed in myself.

Somewhere down the line, I realized that as long as I tried hard and did the best I could do, I should be happy with the grade I earned. It really didn't matter what happened to the other two points — or the other ten for that matter — as long as I had done the best job I could do.

♡ ♡ ♡

Drag your thoughts away from your troubles... by the ears, by the heels, or any other way you can manage it.

♡ *Mark Twain*

I live my life according to that same rule — by living up to the expectations I set for myself, not those that others set for me. It is a good way to live. People may criticize you or put you down throughout life, but the only thing that matters is what you think of yourself. It is hard to live up to other people's expectations, especially those of our parents or teachers. It is a great feeling to make others proud, but more importantly, it is even greater to be able to say you are proud of yourself.

Don't compare yourself to others and don't let anyone else compare you, either. You are and need to be your own person. You do not need to be your sibling, friend, peer, or anyone else. Set goals for yourself that are achievable for you. If you choose to live your life by someone else's guidelines, you may look back on your decisions with regret. Follow your dreams and don't let anyone ever discourage you. Be the best "you" that you can be.

Be a Kid for as Long as You Can...

How much finer it is to go out into the woods and lift up your voice in song, and be a child again, than to fight inclination and waste good God-given energy endeavoring to be proper!

☆ Elbert Hubbard

Having fun doesn't have to end with childhood. Having fun is simply holding on to the joy of each day. It's looking up at the sky and taking a deep breath just because it feels good. It's laughing at the shapes in clouds and dancing in the rain. It's letting go of the "should" voices that tell you that you *should* settle down. It's listening, instead, to the voice inside that says, "...Wouldn't it be fun to stand on your head and wiggle your toes at the sky?"

☆ Judith Harlan

Enjoy the Journey

Time is all we have…
experience fantasies
live the reality
believe in fate
create your destiny
ask questions
seek answers

fall in love
stand in tragedy
get lost
find your own way
face your fears
ignore your weaknesses
make mistakes
resolve your problems
forget yesterday
remember the past
plan ahead
leave something behind
escape time
get caught in the moment
like others
love yourself
age in mind
be young in spirit

read a book
tell a story
reach your destination
enjoy the journey

☆ Jen Barnes, Age 19

What It's All About...

Life isn't about keeping score.
It's not about how many people call you
and it's not about who you've dated,
are dating, or haven't dated at all.
It isn't about who you've kissed,
what sport you play,
or which guy or girl likes you.
It's not about your shoes or your hair
or the color of your skin
or where you live or go to school.
In fact, it's not about grades, money, clothes,
or colleges that accept you or not.
Life isn't about if you have lots of friends,
or if you are alone,
and it's not about how accepted
or unaccepted you are.
Life just isn't about that.

But life is about who you love and who you hurt.
It's about how you feel about yourself.
It's about trust, happiness, and compassion.
It's about sticking up for your friends
and replacing inner hate with love.
Life is about avoiding jealousy,
overcoming ignorance, and building confidence.
It's about what you say and what you mean.
It's about seeing people for who they are
and not what they have.
Most of all, it is about choosing to use your life
to touch someone else's in a way that could never
have been achieved otherwise.
These choices are what life's about.

Author Unknown

ACKNOWLEDGMENTS

We gratefully acknowledge the permission granted by the following authors, publishers, and authors' representatives to reprint poems or excerpts from their publications.

Barbara Cage for "Growing Up Isn't Always Easy." Copyright © 2001 by Barbara Cage. All rights reserved.

Slack Incorporated for "You've got to be real...," "We are already...," "The essence of...," and "Learning is the greatest..." from LIVING, LOVING & LEARNING by Leo Buscaglia. Copyright © 1982 by Leo F. Buscaglia, Inc.

Walker and Company, Inc., for "If your friends...," "Spend time shaping...," "Adults are books...," and "Having fun doesn't..." from GIRL TALK by Judith Harlan. Copyright © 1997 by Judith Harlan.

Beacon Press for "Develop autonomy..." and "Some of the most..." from SELF-PORTRAIT OF A FAMILY by Jessie Bernard. Copyright © 1978 by Jessie Bernard. All rights reserved.

Health Communications, Inc., for "The bottom line..." from TEEN LOVE: ON RELATIONSHIPS by Kimberly Kirberger. Copyright © 1999 by Kimberly Kirberger.

Putnam Berkley, a division of Penguin Putnam, Inc., for "The body is..." and "...Junior high is not..." from REVIVING OPHELIA by Mary Pipher, Ph.D. Copyright © 1994 by Mary Pipher, Ph.D.

Pocket Books, a division of Simon & Schuster, for "Your body is..." from DEAL WITH IT! by Esther Drill, Heather McDonald, and Rebecca Odes. Copyright © 1999 by gURL and Roundtable Press.

Three Rivers Press, a division of Random House, Inc., and Britney Bands, Inc., for "Every girl feels..." from BRITNEY SPEARS' HEART TO HEART by Britney and Lynne Spears with Sheryl Berk. Copyright © 2000 by Lynne Spears and Britney Spears.

The Haworth Press, Inc., for "Women should stop..." from GOOD GIRLS DON'T EAT DESSERT by Rosalyn M. Meadow, Ph.D., and Lillie Weiss, Ph.D. Copyright © 1992 by the Haworth Press, Inc.

Jen Barnes for "Don't judge me..." from "Good Judgment" and "Enjoy the Journey." Copyright © 2001 by Jen Barnes. All rights reserved.

Simon & Schuster and Bonnie M. Parsley for "The part of us..." from THE CHOICE IS YOURS: A TEENAGER'S GUIDE TO SELF-DISCOVERY, RELATIONSHIPS, VALUES, AND SPIRITUAL GROWTH by Bonnie Parsley. Copyright © 1992 by Bonnie Parsley. And for "Life is difficult..." from THE ROAD LESS TRAVELED by M. Scott Peck, M.D. Copyright © 1978 by M. Scott Peck, M.D.

Regnery Publishing, Inc., for "Myself" from THE COLLECTED VERSE OF EDGAR A. GUEST by Edgar A. Guest. Copyright © 1934 by the Reilly & Lee Co.

New World Library for "I want you to know..." from LETTERS TO MY SON by Kent Nerburn. Copyright © 1994 by Kent Nerburn.

S©ott Treimel NY for "I woke up this morning..." from THE ROSE ON MY CAKE by Karla Kuskin. Copyright © 1964 by Karla Kuskin, published by HarperCollins Publishers. Copyright renewed 1992 by Karla Kuskin. All rights reserved.

Veronica A. Shoffstall for "After a While." Copyright © 1971 by Veronica A. Shoffstall. All rights reserved.

Dee Snider and International Creative Management, Inc., for "You feel butterflies..." and "Just because I didn't..." from DEE SNIDER'S TEENAGE SURVIVAL GUIDE by Dee Snider and Philip Bashe, published by Doubleday, a division of Random House, Inc. Copyright © 1987 by Dee Snider.

Songs of Universal, Inc., for "You know you're not..." from the song "(Change Is) Never a Waste of Time" by Alanis Morissette, Leslie Howe, and Serge Cote. Copyright © Songs of Universal, Inc. O/B/O Itself and I Totally Do Music, Universal-MCA Music Publishing, A.D.O. Universal Studios, Inc., O/B/O Itself and Fish or Fudge Songs (ASCAP/BMI). International copyright secured. All rights reserved.

Leeza Azraen for "There will be times..." from "Wishes." Copyright © 2001 by Leeza Azraen. All rights reserved.

Melissa Underwood for "You can't coach heart..." from "The Will to Win." Copyright © 2001 by Melissa Underwood. All rights reserved.

HarperCollins Publishers for "Loosen up..." from MAKE YOUR LIFE WORTH WHILE by Emmet Fox. Copyright © 1942, 1943, 1944, 1945, 1946 by Emmet Fox. Copyright renewed 1974 by Kathleen Whelan. And for "No one can make you..." from THIS IS MY STORY by Eleanor Roosevelt. Copyright © 1937 by Anna Eleanor Roosevelt. Copyright renewed 1965 by Franklin Roosevelt and John Roosevelt.

Kurin Seventh for "Sometimes..." from "Sometimes in Life." Copyright © 2001 by Kurin Seventh. All rights reserved.

Jodi Lynn for "You have to say..." from "This Is My Life." Copyright © 2001 by Jodi Lynn. All rights reserved.

Scripture quotation on page 26 is from the New King James Version. Copyright © 1982 by Thomas Nelson, Inc. All rights reserved.

A careful effort has been made to trace the ownership of selections used in this anthology in order to obtain permission to reprint copyrighted material and give proper credit to the copyright owners. If any error or omission has occurred, it is completely inadvertent, and we would like to make corrections in future editions provided that written notification is made to the publisher:

SPS STUDIOS, INC., P.O. Box 4549, Boulder, Colorado 80306.